THE INSECTO-FILES

Amazing Insect Science and Bug Facts You'll Never Believe

Helaine Becker

Illustrated by Claudia Dávila

MAPLE TREE PRESS

Maple Tree Press books are published by Owlkids Books Inc.
10 Lower Spadina Avenue, Suite 400, Toronto, Ontario M5V 2Z2
www.owlkids.com

Distributed in Canada by Raincoast Books
9050 Shaughnessy Street, Vancouver, British Columbia V6P 6E5

Distributed in the United States by Publishers Group West
1700 Fourth Street, Berkeley, California 94710

Dedication
To the 10 quintillion...

Acknowledgments
Thanks to the Ontario Arts Council for their financial support through the Writers' Reserve program.

Cataloguing in Publication Data

Becker, Helaine, 1961–
      The insecto-files : amazing insect science and bug facts you'll never believe /
Helaine Becker ; illustrated by Claudia Dávila.

Includes index.
ISBN 978-1-897349-46-5 (bound).—ISBN 978-1-897349-47-2 (pbk.)

1. Insects—Juvenile literature. 2. Insects—Experiments—Juvenile literature. I. Dávila, Claudia II. Title.

QL467.2.B42 2009   j595.7   C2008-907538-2

Library of Congress Control Number: 2008910691

Design and illustration: Claudia Dávila

We acknowledge the financial support of the Canada Council for the Arts, the Ontario Arts

OA ONTARIO ARTS COUNCIL
CONSEIL DES ARTS DE L'ONTARIO

Council, the Government of Canada through the Book Publishing Industry Development Program (BPIDP), and the Government of Ontario through the Ontario Media Development Corporation's Book Initiative for our publishing activities.

Printed in China

A   B   C   D   E   F

CONTENTS

ENTER THE INNER INSECT WORLD

Insects are the most numerous creatures on Earth. So far, scientists have identified around 1.8 million species of insects...and they're still counting. Many more are waiting to be discovered. No one really knows how many species there are all together—estimates range from 3 million to 30 million in total! Two out of every three animals on Earth is probably an insect.

Most experts think that there are over 10 quintillion (10,000,000,000,000,000,000) individual insects digging, boring, flying, crawling, and pooping their way in and around the Earth—that's about a billion billion bugs for every single person! And we're not even counting their close relatives, the arachnids, which include spiders, lice, ticks, scorpions, and mites.

In this book, you'll get the chance to investigate insects' out-of-this-world abilities first-hand. So get ready to explore the cool, gross, and fascinating lives of Earth's creepy-crawly critters.

What Makes a Bug a Bug?

All bugs are insects, but not all insects are bugs.

Insects share these common features:

- they **breathe air**

- they have bodies
  with three parts:
  a **head**, a **thorax**,
  and an **abdomen**

- they have **six legs**

- they have an **exoskeleton**, a
  hard shell on the outside of their bodies

Not all insects are exactly alike, though. To make
them easier to study, scientists divide insects into
separate groups, based on their different features.
Beetles, for example, are the group of insects that
have hard wing casings. Butterflies and moths
are in another group. "True bugs" are yet another
grouping, made up of insects that have jointed
beaks that can pierce or suck up fluids. Stink bugs
and bedbugs are true bugs. Ladybugs are not
(they're actually beetles).

In the pages that follow, you'll find loads
of experiments and activities you can do to
help you see into all the inner workings of the
insect world. You can also check out some of
the jaw-dropping experiments that real bug
scientists (entomologists) have performed.

HEAD

THORAX

ABDOMEN

GETTING THE BUG

It's time to meet the neighbors. The insects on this page are common ones you might find at a local park or in your backyard. Do you recognize who's who? Can you match each numbered description to the correct insect picture? (Answers on page 63.)

1 Earwig
These voracious predators have a pair of sharp pincers at their rear end. Earwigs prefer damp conditions and feed on plants and other insects.

2 Stink Bug
These broad, shield-shaped true bugs sport small heads that seem to be "tucked under" their back. They emit a foul smell when threatened.

3 Inchworm
These insects are the larvae of a large group of moths called the Geometridae. They have smooth, hairless bodies and can be green, brown, or black.

4 Aphid
These small, soft-bodied insects are also called plant lice. All aphids have two tubes, called cornicles, on their rear ends, which secrete protective chemicals when attacked.

5 Grasshopper
There are more than 18,000 species of grasshoppers. Most feed on plants. Unlike crickets, which they resemble, grasshoppers are active during the day. Look for long, powerful back legs that enable them to jump up to 75 cm (30 in.).

6 Mosquito larvae
Commonly called "wigglers" or "wrigglers," they can be found hanging under the surface of almost any still water. They move their bodies in an S-shape and dive to the bottom if disturbed.

BASICS

H

I

7 ## Water strider
Also known as pond skaters, these insects are flat, long, and wingless. The second and third pairs of legs are almost twice as long as their bodies.

8 ## Whirligig beetle
These shiny black, oval beetles spin on the water's surface. Their abdomens stick out beyond the wing covers, giving them a distinctive pointy tush.

9 ## Ground beetle
Ground beetles are recognized by their ridged, dark or metallic hardened wing covers. Look for a head that is smaller than the thorax.

What's Not an Insect?
Arachnids are similar to insects, but have three key differences:

• they have bodies with only **two** distinct parts, a **head** and an **abdomen**
• they have **eight legs**
• they **don't have** antennae

Spiders, ticks, and scorpions are all arachnids.

SPOT THE FAKERS QUIZ

Check out the bugs below. Can you figure out which one is the true insect? (See answer on page 63.)

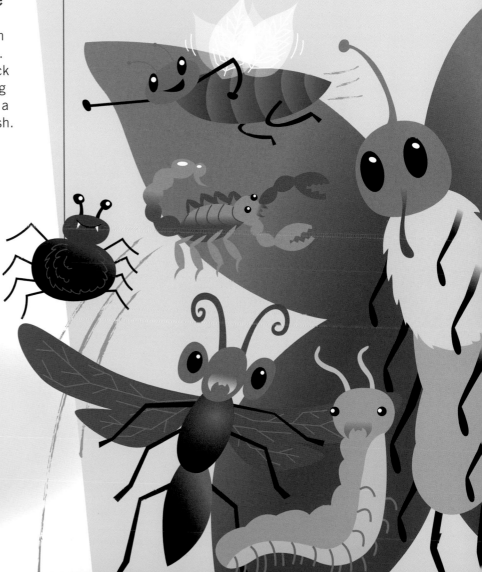

A BUG'S GOT TO EAT

They may be small, but their appetites are not. Insects love to eat, after all. Think of any substance, and there's probably a bug that will happily devour it: fruit, stems, roots, other insects, glue, even your dandruff!

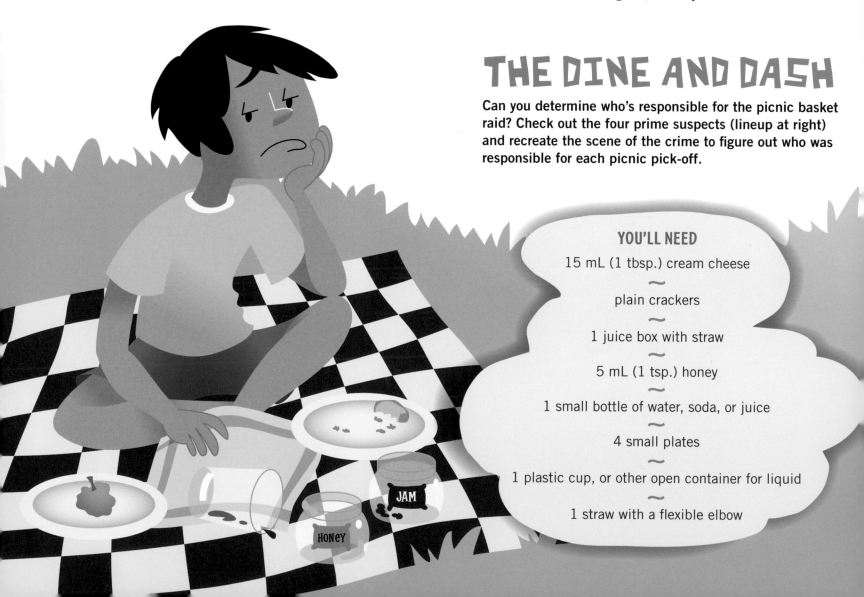

THE DINE AND DASH

Can you determine who's responsible for the picnic basket raid? Check out the four prime suspects (lineup at right) and recreate the scene of the crime to figure out who was responsible for each picnic pick-off.

YOU'LL NEED

15 mL (1 tbsp.) cream cheese

~

plain crackers

~

1 juice box with straw

~

5 mL (1 tsp.) honey

~

1 small bottle of water, soda, or juice

~

4 small plates

~

1 plastic cup, or other open container for liquid

~

1 straw with a flexible elbow

Gus "The Gastronome"
Grasshopper

Fiona "Four-Eyes"
Fly

Avidia "The Sharp" Aphid

"Lefty" Lepidoptera

1 In this activity, each of the four plates represents a different type of food. Put the cream cheese on one plate. Stick a cracker in the cheese so it stands upright.

2 Put the juice box on another plate.

3 Put the honey on a third plate.

4 Open the bottle of water, soda, or juice. Pour out three quarters of the liquid into another container and set it aside. Put the bottle on the fourth plate.

5 Using only your teeth, try and eat each of the different foods. Keep your hands behind your back.

6 Now, still without using your hands, try to lap up the different foods using nothing but your tongue.

7 This time, try to eat each of the four foods using the short straw from the juice box.

8 Finally, use the flexible straw to try each of the four foods.

What's Going On?

Did you figure out which mouth parts work best with each type of food? To see which of the four foods each insect might prefer, here's the "bite" on each of the felon's mouth parts:

- Insects such as **grasshoppers** or **caterpillars** have jaws that can bite off and chew food.
- **Flies** have long feeding tubes. A spongy tip at the end soaks up liquidy foods.
- **True bugs** such as aphids pierce the outer surface of plants to get at the liquid sap inside it.
- **Butterflies** have a long feeding tube, or proboscis, that they unfurl and insert into flowers to suck up the nectar inside.

Check your answers on page 63.

FEEDING FRENZY

Who knew those tiny mouthparts could be so powerful?

Crunchy on the Outside

About 80% of predatory insects, as well as arachnids, can't chew their food. They can only suck up liquids. But the insects they eat have a solid shell with firm flesh inside. So how do they get at their tasty meal? Using fangs called stylets, the insects puncture their preys' exoskeleton. They then inject saliva containing enzymes that dissolve the prey's insides. Now they can suck up the goo inside. Slurp!

The cabbage butterfly has a special taste organ just for mustard (a member of the cabbage family)!

Aw yeah, now we're talkin'!

Try It!

Use an eyedropper to drip warm water on a sugar cube. Does the cube start to melt? The water acts like the insects' saliva to break down the solid sugar into a liquid.

Captains of Crunch

Most carnivorous insects suck the guts out of their victims, but some eat their prey whole. Without teeth, how can these insects grind up the tough, crunchy exoskeletons? Insects have an organ called the gizzard, or proventriculus, which is lined with toothlike plates that grind and crush the food. A second set of plates is covered with short, fine hairs. The hairs act as a filter to strain out any remaining large chunks before the mashed food continues on its way.

BEWARE THE BITE

Insects, like mosquitoes, that have stabbing mouthparts not only deliver a painful bite, they can also transfer diseases. Do this investigation to see how.

1 Fill each bowl with water.

2 Add several drops of food coloring to one bowl. Mix. The color should be solid.

3 Squeeze the bulb of the turkey baster. Place the tip of the baster into the colored liquid.

4 Release the bulb to suck some colored liquid into the baster.

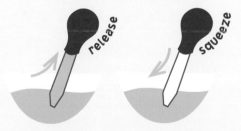

5 Squeeze again, squirting the liquid back into the SAME container.

6 Next, repeat steps 3 to 5 with the bowl of plain water. Squirt it back into the SAME container.

7 Carefully study the color of the water in the clear container. Do you see traces of the color from the other bowl? How did the color get into the plain water? Does this help to show how insects like flies and mosquitoes can transfer diseases?

What's Going On?

Every time a fly or mosquito bites, it sucks up liquid from its host. But not all of the liquid leaves its stinger. A small amount of residue remains behind. Some of this residue can be transferred to the next animal the insect bites. If the residue contains disease-causing organisms, like the parasite that causes malaria, the insect can infect host after host after host.

11

SUPER-SIZED INSECTS?

Does the thought of an insect the size of a tractor-trailer give you the willies?
Breathe easy...insects and arachnids can't grow much bigger than they already are.
Not anymore, anyway.

Dino-Mite?

Insects in the time of *T. rex* were not only plentiful, but they were big. A prehistoric dragonfly might have had the wingspan of a hawk. That's about four times wider than that of the largest modern dragonfly! So—*gulp*—why aren't insects horror-movie big today? Believe it or not, some of it has to do with the air (see page 14).

But for the most part, it's what's inside that counts. Insects don't have bones inside their bodies. Instead, they are covered with a hard exoskeleton. The exoskeleton is made of a material similar to that of your fingernails, called chitin. It is very versatile, and can be either stiff and strong, like a stag beetle's shell, or flexible and transparent, like a butterfly's wing.

When an insect is small, the chitin exoskeleton is thin and light. As an insect gets bigger, however, its shell gets thicker and heavier in order to support its weight. An insect the size of, say, you, would have such a thick shell there'd be no room inside it for its body parts—so it simply couldn't be. Phew!

How Old Is Old?

Insects and arachnids may have been among the very first animals to live on land! The oldest-known insects were identified from a fossilized insect jaw. It had been stored in a collection at a museum in England since 1928. In 2004, researchers accidentally stumbled across the sample. They realized it was the remains of an ancient winged insect, and that the sample dated back over **400 million years ago**! That's more than 200 million years before the first dinosaurs were even on the scene!

EEK! A bug!!

BZZZZZZZZZZZZZZZ

Try It!

Take a good look at the width of this page. Now picture a dragonfly spreading its wings across it. The dragonfly with the largest wingspan living today is the *Megaloprepus coerulatus* (say that ten times fast!). It lives in Central America. Its wings measure a whopping 19 cm (7½ in.) from tip to tip—almost as wide as this page!

13

SIZING THEM UP

You've just read about the limitations of chitin and insect growth. Another reason why bugs can't super-size has to do with oxygen. When you breathe, you take oxygen from the air into your lungs. Insects, however, don't have lungs. So *how* do they breathe?

How Big Is Too Big?

A recent study conducted at Midwestern University in Arizona looked at how large a modern insect can grow and still get enough oxygen to live. They came up with a maximum body length of about 15 cm (6 in.). That turns out to be the average size of the largest-known insect today, South America's **Titanic Longhorn Beetle.**

Dino-Air

Insects get oxygen from the air through tiny pores in their exoskeleton called spiracles. The spiracles connect to a network of air tubes that delivers oxygen directly to the cells. Since there is no pump to move oxygen around, the insect needs plenty of spiracles to take enough air into its body.

Thanks to a miracle of math, the larger an object grows, the smaller its relative surface area becomes. It has a smaller amount of "skin" (and, therefore, spiracles) compared to the volume of its "guts." With their relatively smaller exoskeletons, insects that grow too big cannot take in enough oxygen to survive.

So how could ancient dino-bugs grow dino-big? In prehistoric times, Earth's atmosphere contained 14% more oxygen than it does today. The richer air made it easier for insects to get oxygen, which meant they could grow quite a bit larger.

GO WITH THE FLOW

The flow of air into an insect's body is controlled by small muscles around the openings of the spiracles. They contract, or tighten, to close the spiracle, and relax to open it. Do this air-raising activity to catch spiracles in action.

YOU'LL NEED

large bug (a caterpillar works well)

~

magnifying glass or magnifying bug viewer (see page 60)

1 Capture a large insect.

2 Use a magnifying glass or bug viewer to examine the insect. Can you see tiny openings along the sides of its thorax and abdomen? Most insects usually have one pair of spiracles per body segment.

3 Watch one spiracle closely. Do you see it open and close?

4 When you have finished studying the insect, release it gently in the same place you captured it.

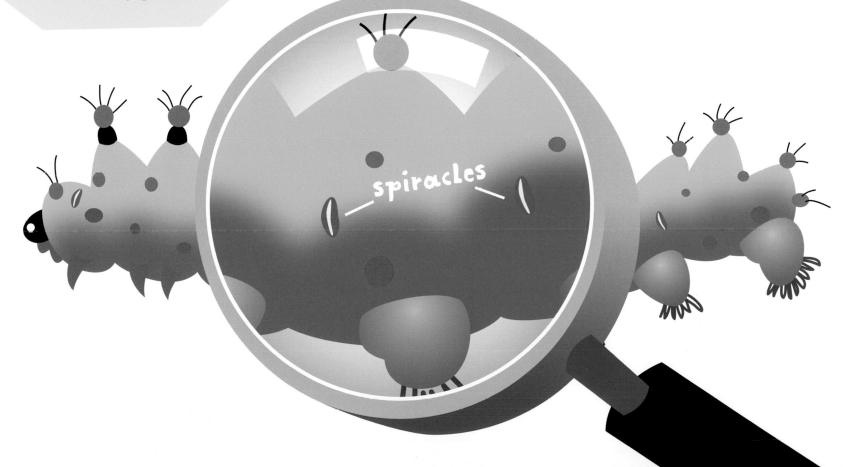

spiracles

CREATURES OF THE NIGHT

Have you ever noticed that when the sun goes down,
lots of insects come out to play?

Can't...
resist...
the light!

Lepidoptera is the scientific
name for the group of insects
that includes butterflies
and moths.

Night Lights

You've probably seen moths and other nocturnal insects
crashing into bright lights. Have you ever wondered why? For
nocturnal insects, the only natural light is normally the moon
and stars. To a moth, therefore, bright lights in the sky should
be too far away to ever touch.

Many scientists think that a bright artificial light messes up
moths' steering systems. They believe moths actually use the
moon to guide them as they fly. If the moths see a bright light,
they might think it's the moon, and use it to set their course,
instead of the real moon. BONK! Talk about seeing stars!

Once a moth comes close to the light, it probably becomes
temporarily blind, much the way you do when you step from a
dark room into a brightly lit one. Blinded by the light, it can't
find its way back in the dark. Even worse, the moth has only
a tiny short term memory. By the time it can see again you've
got a luckless Lepidoptera that's already forgotten that the
light isn't the moon. Smack! Smack! Smack! Sizzle....

Straight to the Moon!

Some moths may also use a special trick to avoid predators. When they sense danger, all the moths in a shrub fly up in the air at the same time. To a moth, "up" always means "toward the moon." So now imagine you are a moth that's in danger. You fly up—and smash right into the porch light!

Try It!

Most insects can't see the color red. Cover the end of a flashlight with some red cellophane. Keep very quiet and still as you shine the red light on your subjects. With a little luck, the insects won't react to your presence, and you'll get a spy's-eye view of night sprites at work.

A LIGHT IN THE DARK

Use this simple technique to observe and capture stealthy insects that operate under the cloak of darkness.

YOU'LL NEED

white bedsheet

~

string, thumbtacks, or other fasteners

~

porch light or flashlight

1 Ask a parent for a white sheet they don't mind you taking outside.

2 Use the string or tacks to hang the sheet under the porch light or from the branches of a tree, where the light can shine on it.

3 Turn on the porch light or flashlight and observe.

4 Night-flying insects will be attracted to the light, and you should soon see them cling to the sheet. Observe them on the sheet or capture them with your touchless bug catcher (page 61).

What's Going On?

Your light-and-sheet combination acts as a lure to nocturnal insects attracted to light. While it's "enlightening" to observe night insects with this technique, keep in mind that you are not watching the insects' normal evening activities.

THE INSECTO-FILES

AMAZING BUG FACTS

FIZZZZZZ!

Stop blaming it on the dog: insect flatulence (burps and toots, to you and me) counts for 20% of the world's emissions of methane gas!

When a species of grasshopper called *Romalea microptera* is in danger, it produces a foul-smelling, brown froth. The froth stops even its hardiest predators, such as ants. When scientists analyzed the substance, they discovered it contained 2,5-dichlorophenol, a chemical found only in a **man-made weedkiller**! The grasshoppers can eat plants sprayed with the deadly chemical, but ants won't go near the plants. The grasshoppers incorporate the poison into their own defense system to keep ants away from them, too.

Entomophobia is the unfounded fear of bugs. About one out of every ten people suffer from this syndrome.

Oh no, you've cut your finger and need stitches. Thank goodness for **bug bits**! Many surgical sutures are made from chitin, the same material that gives insect exoskeletons their strength and flexibility. Chitin stitches are strong enough to keep surgical wounds closed up tight. Plus, because they dissolve completely over time, the stitches don't need to be taken out once a patient is healed—they just disappear. Thanks for the inspiration, bugs!

If you want to keep mosquitoes away, consider rubbing some catnip under your arms. Yeah, your cat Fluffy may go wild; mosquitoes, on the other hand, will head for the hills. According to the American Chemical Society, **mosquitoes loathe catnip**! They hate it so much that it's about ten times more effective than DEET, the most commonly used insect repellant.

LOVE is iN THE AiR

Fireflies use mood lighting to find and attract mates. Other insects use different romantic techniques. Ready to be a fly on the wall and see how some insects find their match?

INSTANT MESSAGING FIREFLY STYLE

Fireflies are not actually flies, but beetles. To test your own skill in communicating like a firefly, perform this role-playing game with your "brightest" pals.

1 Divide the players into two groups—one will be male, the other female. Give each male firefly a flashlight.

2 Secretly give each female a letter A or B. Assign each letter its own flash pattern. (Example: group A has three short flashes; group B, two long flashes.)

3 Tear the paper into the same number of pieces as you have males. Write "A: three short flashes" on half, and "B: two long flashes" on the remaining half. Fold the papers and mix them up.

4 Have each male choose a piece of paper from the pile. Make sure everybody keeps his or her identity secret!

5 Have all the female fireflies sit in a circle. Then have the male fireflies walk around the circle, flashing their lights in the assigned pattern. When one of the females recognizes a male with her flash pattern, she can jump up and tap him on the shoulder. Time how long it takes for everyone pair off.

YOU'LL NEED

4 or more players
~
a flashlight for half of the players
~
writing paper
~
pencil

What's Going On?

Fireflies have an organ called a lantern on the lower tip of their abdomens that can flash. They use a particular pattern of flashes to attract prey or mates. Each firefly species has its own flash pattern, so fireflies know how to find one of their own kind to mate with and carry on the species.

Bright Lights

Fireflies make their light shine bright through a chemical reaction. The glowing cells in their abdomen contain a chemical called luciferin. The luciferin combines with another chemical to produce an enzyme called luciferase. When luciferase mixes with oxygen, it produces a cool, pale light, usually yellow to reddish green in color. In addition, the light-producing cells contain crystals of a substance called uric acid. The crystals reflect light, making the firefly's glow even brighter.

Energy Efficient

Fireflies are cool, but not only because they can flash like mini-stars. Think about a lit lightbulb. Lightbulbs are not cool. They get hot. That's because only a small part of the energy they consume is used to produce light. The rest—almost 90% of it!—is wasted as unwanted heat. A perfect light would use every last bit of energy it consumes to make light, with nothing wasted. And that's just what fireflies produce—a cool, energy-efficient perfect light.

Try It!

With more than 170 species across North America, fireflies may be common where you live. If so, you'll find it a breeze to catch fireflies at dusk on a warm summer evening. Look for males cruising a few feet above the ground. Females will be lurking in low vegetation nearby. Catch the fireflies with your cupped hands—carefully so you don't squash the bugs—and put them in a glass jar. Cover the jar opening with foil, with small holes poked through for air. Enjoy the glow of your firefly lantern, then release them unharmed.

At times, fireflies change their flash patterns. Why? They might want to trick other fireflies into thinking they are responding to one of their own species.

L♥VE SONGS

Fireflies may have the edge when it comes to mood lighting, but they're not the only insects with a romantic side. Meet the crooners of the insect world: crickets and grasshoppers.

SCRATCH ME A TUNE

Male crickets sing love songs to their would-be honeys. They don't use their mouths to sing their tune, though. They use their wings to chirp. See if you can get the female crickets to come calling with this experiment.

YOU'LL NEED

2 pieces of rough sandpaper, long enough to wrap around your arms and approximately 10 cm (4 in.) wide

~

4 elastic bands

1 Wrap a sheet of the sandpaper around one of your forearms.

2 Secure the sandpaper around your arm with two elastics to hold it in place.

3 Repeat on the other side to make a second sandpaper armband.

4 Rub your arms together to make a rasping sound. You've just said "I love you" in cricket-ese!

What's Going On?

On the top of each wing, there is a pair of rough scrapers called a rasp and file. When the two wings are rubbed together, they make a distinctive chirping sound.

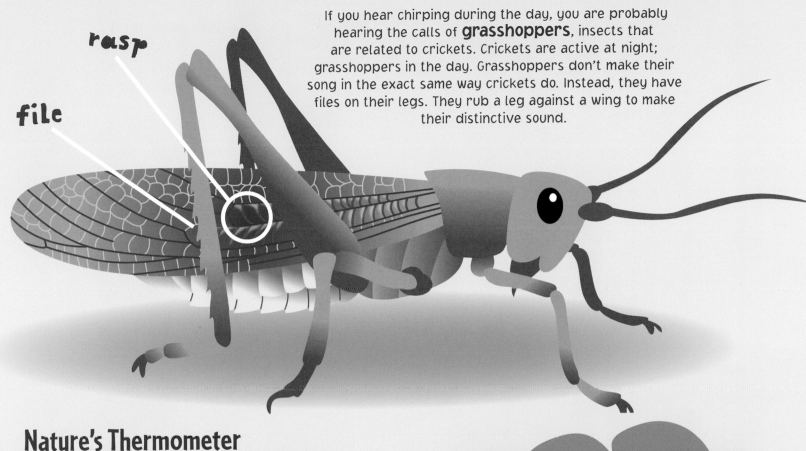

rasp

file

If you hear chirping during the day, you are probably hearing the calls of **grasshoppers**, insects that are related to crickets. Crickets are active at night; grasshoppers in the day. Grasshoppers don't make their song in the exact same way crickets do. Instead, they have files on their legs. They rub a leg against a wing to make their distinctive sound.

Nature's Thermometer

The pitch of the cricket's tune doesn't change—each sound it makes is exactly the same tone as every other. But the rhythm of the tune can vary quite a bit. How quickly each chirp follows another sends important information to the female. It can tell the female about what species is calling, and how healthy the singer is. Cricket chirps also change with the temperature. The warmer the night, the faster the cricket will chirp.

Try It!

You can actually measure the temperature by counting a cricket's chirps. To make your own cricket thermometer, just do the math! Listen for the chirps of a cricket on a summer evening. Using a clock with a second hand, count the number of chirps you hear in 8 seconds. Add 3. The result is the temperature in degrees Celsius.

L♥VE SCENTS

Do you think love stinks? Insects do—but in a good way. B.O. (body odor) is beautiful if you're a bug. They often rely on their sense of smell to find the perfect partner.

Ooh la la!

Smells Like Love

Moths and butterflies find their mates by sniffing chemicals called pheromones in the air. These pheromones are very powerful. Male emperor moths can detect female moth pheromones from as far away as 11 km (7 mi.).

When the female of the species is ready to lay her eggs, she gives off a distinctive perfume from the tip of her abdomen. As she flies, the perfume streams out behind her. The male's antennae are equipped with sensors that are very sensitive to the female's scent. When it detects a female pheromone molecule in the air, the male flies toward the source of the aroma. If the scent weakens, the moth knows he's heading the wrong way. He turns around and zigzags the other way. He goes back and forth, back and forth, always heading toward the scent. The stronger the scent, the closer he is to the female. With a little luck, he'll find her soon, and their courtship will begin.

THE POLKA-DOT HOT SPOT

Did you know that even flies have a weakness for romance? Set up a fake fly party, complete with decoy flies, and see how many you can attract to your polka-dot hot spot.

YOU'LL NEED

2 sheets of paper

~

fly bait, such as a small amount of honey (optional)

~

black marker

~

notepad and pencil

1
Make a polka-dot pattern on one sheet of paper. Use your marker to draw 10 random dots, about 1 cm (½ in.) apart. Make each dot about the size of a fly.

2
Place the paper on the ground or on a table in a sunny location where you've seen flies. You may need to hold the paper in place with some pebbles at each corner.

3
Observe your fly spots for 15 minutes. Do any flies visit your spotty hot spot? How many? Keep a record of what kind of insects and how many individuals visit your phony flies.

4
Now lay a second sheet of blank paper nearby. Place a few dabs of honey on both sheets of paper. Observe both for 15 minutes. Do more flies visit the polka dot or the plain paper?

Try It!
You can try using a different number or arrangement of polka dots to see if you observe any differences in fly behavior.

What's Going On?
Flies are attracted to each other primarily by sight. A black spot on white paper appears to be a potential mate to a hovering fly. But what happened when you sweetened the spot with some honey? Did you observe more flies coming to the plain paper with honey, or was the real fly party where there were both honey and mates?

EYE is FOR iNSECT

Are you ready for a bug-eyed view of the world? Here's everything you need to know about insecto-vision.

WHAT THE FLY SAW

You hear a buzzing sound near your ear. You are under fly-by surveillance. Swat! Miss. Swat! Miss. Swat! Miss. The fly evades you again and again. How does the fly see you coming every time?

YOU'LL NEED

2 pencils

1 Hold the pencils in front of you horizontally at arm's length.

2 Close one eye.

3 Move the pencils toward one another and touch the tips together. Do the pencils appear oddly flat? Did you misjudge their distance?

4 Now try the same experiment again with both eyes open. Is it easier to touch the pencils together?

What's Going On?

Your eyes are placed so that what each eye sees is slightly different. There is an area directly in front of you where what each eye sees overlaps. Your brain takes these two images and fuses them together so that you can tell how far away objects are. This ability is called stereoscopic vision. Large-eyed insects, such as flies, also have superb stereoscopic vision. Would a fly be able to avoid predators so well if it did not have stereoscopic vision?

EYES IN THE BACK OF YOUR HEAD

Large-eyed insects can see nearly the entire way around their heads—to their front, sides, and rear! This makes it pretty hard to sneak up on a fly. To get a fly's eye view, build your own 3-D visual-simulation monitor (you can call them "Fly-Specks").

YOU'LL NEED

1 pair inexpensive plastic sunglasses

~

cardboard rectangle, 5 cm (2 in.) x 15 cm (6 in.)

~

2 flexible plastic mirrors (available at arts or science supply stores), cut to approximately 5 cm (2 in.) square

~

ruler

~

pencil

~

duct tape

~

white glue

1 Pop out the lenses of the glasses.

2 Place the cardboard on your work surface with the long edge closest to you.

3 Use your pencil to score (cutting a line *into* but *not through* the cardboard) two parallel lines in the cardboard, each equidistant from the long edges. Your cardboard should now be divided into three equal sections.

4 Fold the cardboard on both lines. The two edges should meet to make a pyramid. Tape securely.

5 Glue one mirror to one face of the pyramid. Glue the second mirror to a second face of the pyramid. Let dry.

6 Put a thick blob of glue on the bridge of the glasses. Find the edge of the pyramid where the two mirrors meet. Press this edge into the glue on the glasses. Hold firmly in place.

7 Wrap tape around the bridge of the glasses and tape the pyramid in place. The tape should stick well to the bare cardboard inside the pyramid.

8 Put on the glasses. You should be able to see all around you!

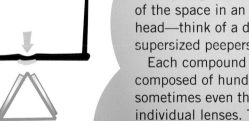

What's Going On?

The glasses mimic how large-eyed bugs' compound eyes see—with full 3-D, front, side, and rear view! Up to 80% of an insect's brain is devoted to processing information from its eyes and antennae—its most important sense organs.

Insects have two different types of eyes. The first, called ocelli, are very simple. They detect changes in light levels. There are usually three ocelli, arranged in a triangle on the top or front of the head.

The other type of eye is called a compound eye. Insects usually have two compound eyes. They can be very large, taking up most of the space in an insect's head—think of a dragonfly's supersized peepers.

Each compound eye is composed of hundreds—sometimes even thousands—of individual lenses. The images from all the lenses combine in the insect's brain to make a single picture of the world.

EH? What's that you say?

HEAR! HEAR!

Insects rely on keen hearing to sense danger, locate prey, and find mates. They have four different types of hearing organs. Tympana are the most common. Different insects have tympana in different places. In grasshoppers, they are on the thorax. In crickets, you can see them on the front legs. Lacewings have tympana on their wings.

MAKE YOUR OWN INSECT TYMPANUM

YOU'LL NEED

plastic wrap
~
30–40 grains of uncooked rice
~
large metal or ceramic bowl

1 Stretch the plastic wrap across the top of the bowl. Stick it to the sides of the bowl, making sure it is firmly attached and the surface is flat and very tight.

2 Put the grains of rice on top of the plastic wrap.

3 Bring your lips up close to (but not touching) the side of the bowl and hum loudly. What happens when you make a very loud sound? Do the grains of rice jump around?

A second type of hearing organ is called **Johnston's Organ**. Flies and mosquitoes have this nifty gadget—particularly sensitive to the sound of a potential mate's wing beats—at the base of their antennae.

What's Going On?

Tympana have a thick membrane that is stretched across an opening. When sound waves hit the membrane, the membrane vibrates, just as the plastic wrap did in the experiment (that's what caused the rice to move). The vibrations are picked up by nerve cells. Nerves then transmit the information to the insect's brain. Its brain "hears" what the tympana felt—the motion of the air produced by sound waves. Your eardrums work exactly the same way!

Who's the Loudest of Them All?

Male cicadas' mating calls have been recorded at up to 120 decibels. That's louder than a lawn mower! To make the sound, cicadas have a pair of ridged, stiff membranes called tymbals at the base of the abdomen. When the cicadas contract the muscles around the tymbals, the membranes buckle inward and make a popping sound, something like what happens when you unscrew the lid of a vacuum-sealed jar. When the cicada relaxes the same muscles, the tymbals return to their original position. Cicadas can contract and relax the tymbals more than 100 times a second, producing a continuous, shrill love poem.

I *Bzzz* You!

In a recent study conducted by two British scientists, the whine of mosquito wings turned out to be a love song! They found that male and female mosquitoes will actually change the rate at which they beat their wings to match the rate of a potential mate. They do this by listening to the pitch of the sound made by their wing flaps. The faster the wing flaps, the higher pitched the whine!

The researchers say that while many other animals recognize the opposite sex by the sounds they make, this is the first time any insect has been shown to change its tune in response to sound. Still unknown, though, is how this whiny behavior helps mosquitoes mate.

Try It!

Many insects can hear vibrations passing through the ground. Stamp on the ground near an ant nest. Wait a few minutes. Do the ants come out of the nest to find the source of the noise?

The pilifer is a hearing organ located in some species of moths. It is designed to hear the echolocation calls of bats. Since bats feed on moths, this sense organ is very helpful for avoiding becoming bat supper. When the moth hears the clicking of the bat's echolocation, it drops from the air or changes its flight path.

Now where did that moth go?

SMALL BUT MIGHTY

Don't be fooled. Insects may be small in stature, but they are equipped with some powerful weapons. Here's how some of the toughest insects defeat their enemies.

THE DEADLY BARB

When a bee stings, it's a kamikaze tactic to protect the hive. A bee is unlikely to sting unless it thinks its colony is in danger, because while its barbed stinger inflicts a painful wound in its victim, it also causes the bee's guts to rip loose from its body. See the action of a bee's barb first-hand with this twisted simulation.

The bee's **stinger** only sticks in the flesh of birds and mammals. The barbs easily penetrate the chitin of other insects and can slip free without killing the bee!

YOU'LL NEED

styrofoam block
(about a 15 cm / 6 in. cube)

~

1 straight nail

~

1 screw-in type hook

1 Use your thumb to push the nail into the foam. Does it go in easily?

2 Now, using your fingers, pull the nail out. Does it come out of the foam easily?

3 Next, insert the threaded end of the hook into the styrofoam. Twist the hook to make it go in.

4 Without twisting, pull the hook from the foam. Is it as easy to remove? If you succeed in pulling it out, what happens to the styrofoam hole? Is it smooth or torn up?

What's Going On?

The nail is shaped like a wasp's stinger. It goes in and out of flesh easily. The screw is shaped like the barb on a bee's stinger. The barbed stinger causes more damage to tissue than a straight stinger does, and is also harder to remove. When a bee stings, its barb sticks in the victim, and the bee is forced to leave its stinger behind.

BAMMO!

The explosive bombardier beetle stores its chemical weapons in its abdomen. When threatened, the beetle lets the two chemicals mix, producing—BAM!—a highly explosive chemical reaction. A nozzle at the tip of its abdomen shoots boiling hot spray at its attacker. Prepare yourself for an encounter by creating an explosive spray of your own.

Note: You will need adult supervision for this activity. It's messy, so consider doing it outdoors.

YOU'LL NEED

125 mL (½ cup) vinegar

~

30 mL (2 tbsp.) baking soda

~

small plastic soda bottle

~

small square of tissue

~

measuring cup and spoons

1 Pour the vinegar into the bottle.

2 Place the bottle in a secure place, such as buried to the neck in dirt or wedged between two bricks. Make sure its neck is pointing straight up in the air.

3 Place the baking soda onto the tissue. Fold the tissue into a small bundle. It should fit into the neck of the bottle.

4 Stuff the tissue with the baking soda inside it into the bottle so it drops into the vinegar.

5 Step back at least a metre (3 ft.). Watch as the two chemicals mix and produce a plume of spray!

What's Going On?

Inside the abdomen of a bombardier beetle, two glands produce two different chemicals. When the beetle feels threatened, the chemicals are forced into a heart-shaped reaction chamber where cells secrete chemicals called enzymes. These enzymes set a series of chemical reactions in motion. The end result is yet another chemical, the highly irritating tongue twister p-benzoquinones. The reaction also produces lots of oxygen and enough heat to boil water.

When you mix baking soda and vinegar, you cause a chemical reaction similar to the beetle's spray. These two chemicals react to produce lots of carbon dioxide, the gas that gives the oomph to your explosion. Carbon dioxide gas also forces the liquid out of the beetle's anus, in the same way it made the liquid shoot out of your soda bottle.

THE INSECTO-FILES

AMAZING BUG FACTS

Many insects make sounds that we cannot hear. The sounds are called **supersonic**—above our range of hearing. These sounds vibrate at a frequency of more than 20,000 vibrations each second.

The aptly named stink bug releases a chemical called an aldehyde from its posterior. Strangely enough, in small doses, aldehydes are the base for some of the world's loveliest perfumes! Slap on too much aldehyde, though, and that perfume turns putrid. **A stink bug's odor is so bad**, if one is put into a cage without enough ventilation, it can even kill itself!

EAU DE STINK BUG

When Brazilian scientists tried to create a hardier, yet gentle, warm-weather bee that would thrive in South America, they imported an African species of honeybee to cross-breed with the European honeybee. Unfortunately, some of the African bees escaped into the wild. There, they bred with native bees to form an aggressive new species. Africanized honeybees (or **killer bees** as they came to be known) spread quickly up through Mexico, and into the United States. The killer bee has been portrayed as a horrible, deadly monster. But while they are more likely to attack and sting than regular bees, they are in fact not more venomous than regular bees.

I'm not that bad, honest!

Periodical cicadas have the longest lifespan of any insect. In a miracle of timing, the grubs all mature together, so that every adult emerges from its pupae at the same time every 17 years. Unfortunately for them, a certain **fanny-loving fungus** that causes the rear ends of the cicadas to fall off also emerges every 17 years. A few species of periodic cicadas, however, have evolved to have a shorter life span—only 13 years—perhaps to avoid the deadly fungus.

33

LOCO LOCOMOTION

It's not easy to keep up with this league of hopping, crawling, flying, leaping fellas. Find out how some of the most agile members of the Order of the Insect get around.

STICKY FEET

You've seen flies walk up the walls. But these sneaks can also walk upside down—on the ceiling! How do they do it?

YOU'LL NEED

1 sheet tracing paper

~

1 sheet paper

~

15 mL (1 tbsp.) water

~

drinking glass

~

pencil

~

scissors

1 Lay the tracing paper on the picture on page 35. Trace the outline. Cut out.

2 Trace the shape onto the paper and cut out. Fold the cut-out shape on the dotted line.

3 Bend the tips of your fly feet up so they can sit flat on a table.

4 Dip your finger tip in the water. Dampen all six feet.

5 Hold the glass in one hand. With the other hand, turn the fly so the feet are pointing up.

6 Press the feet against the bottom of the glass. Let go. Does your fly stick to the glass?

What's Going On?

Water molecules tend to adhere, or stick to, other water molecules. Think about how a wet glass sticks on a tabletop. The water molecules on the bottom of the glass adhere to the water molecules on the table. A fly's feet have pads between the claws that are designed to take advantage of water's stickiness. That's right—they're wet! When the wet pads touch a surface, they act just like the bottom of the glass. The water molecules on them stick to the now wet surface. Hairs all over the pads increase the contact area, making for a very sticky pad indeed. Their stick factor is so strong it can even overcome the force of gravity—and yet not so sticky that they get glued to the spot hanging upside-down!

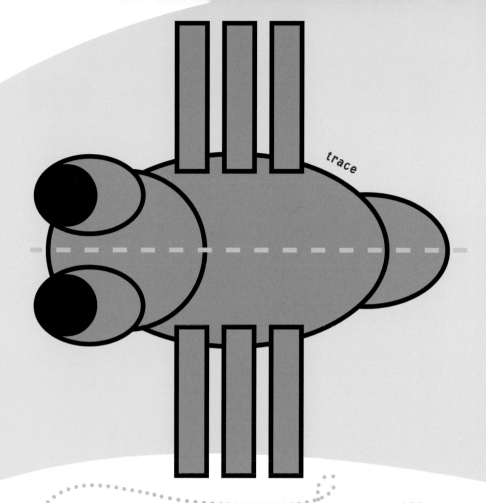

trace

Try It!

Wet the bottom of a glass. Rub it on a smooth surface, like a kitchen counter. Then try to lift it straight up. Does it stick?

Size and Stickiness

Wish you could walk on the ceiling? A team of scientists has designed a robot that might lead the way! The scientists attached a furry, man-made material to the bottom of a robot's feet. The researchers then taught the robot to gently peel its sticky foot off a surface just as a fly does. Can the robot help you walk on the ceiling? Only if you can shrink to the size of a fly. Sticky as the robot feet are, they are not sticky enough to overcome gravity's pull on a full-sized human. The amount of stickiness needed to hold you upside-down would be too much to allow you to peel off.

35

WALKING ON WATER?

Have you ever been surprised to see an insect striding towards you across the water?
How do they do that without sinking?

MEET WALTER S. TRIDER

Walter S. Trider can walk on water—literally. You'll need a needle to tease out Walter's tried-and-true method.

YOU'LL NEED

a sewing needle
(should be clean
and dry)
~
glass of water

Water striders can **leap into the air** to avoid predators, such as fish, or to avoid drowning during a rain storm. The water's skin acts like a springy trampoline to cushion each leap.

1 Gently lay the needle lengthwise on the surface of the water.

2 Carefully watch what the needle does. Does it sink, or float on the water's surface like a water strider?

The **giant** Vietnamese water strider measures a hefty 20 cm (8 in.) long, yet can still walk on water.

What's Going On?

You already know that water molecules attract other water molecules (see page 35). On the water's surface, the molecules are attracted to those beneath them. The pull is so strong that a kind of skin is formed. A light object, like the needle or a water strider, can rest on the skin without breaking it. Water striders are also helped by fine hairs on their legs that trap air bubbles. The air bubbles repel water, helping the strider stay at the surface.

Bouncy, Bouncy Rubber... Flea?

Water striders bounce on water thanks to hairy feet. Fleas get their bounce from a protein called resilin. This amazingly rubbery material can be stretched to three times its length without breaking. It can also be squeezed into a tight ball. Imagine a rubber ball (a resilin pad) embedded in the "thigh," or coxa, of a flea. When the flea bends its leg, the resilin is squeezed. When the flea straightens its leg, the resilin bounces back to its original shape, releasing a large burst of energy. That energy allows the leg to snap open very quickly. The fast snap of the legs is exactly what a flea needs to get off the ground. The faster the snap, the higher the jump. Some fleas can jump 100 times their height, or about 20 cm (8 in.) off the ground.

Scientists in Australia have figured out how to make artificial resilin. They copied a gene for resilin from a fruit fly and inserted it into the gene for a kind of bacteria. The bacteria started acting like a factory, pumping out resiln when they were exposed to light. The man-made resilin might have many uses: to repair damaged blood vessels, to perform spinal disc implants, or even to make super-springy heels for running shoes.

Scubugs

Not all insects stay on the surface of the water. But insects are air-breathing. So how do pond-dwelling insects survive underwater?

air bubble

The predacious diving beetle grabs an **air bubble** and traps it under its wing covers. Then it dives to the bottom to get its food until it uses up its air supply.

snorkel

Many insect larvae have **gills** that allow them to take oxygen directly from the water. But mosquito larvae breathe through a **snorkel-like tube** that sticks up above the surface of the water.

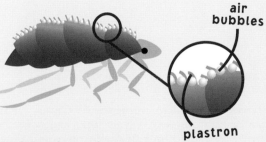

air bubbles

plastron

The water bug *Aphelocheirus*'s body is covered with a dense layer of hairs called a **plastron**. Air bubbles stick to the plastron, so the insect is completely covered with a **layer of air** as it swims.

Some insect larvae have yet another ingenious method for getting oxygen. They thrust their **spiracles** into the air-filled pockets of some aquatic plants.

Six-legged water striders have one pair of very long legs—the middle pair—and two pairs of short, stubby ones. While the stubby front and back legs keep the insect afloat, the middle legs act as oars to **propel the strider** forward.

THE CREEPY CRAWLERS

They may not have the bounce of a flea or the spring in their step that a water strider has,
but creepy-crawly caterpillars can still get around!

Hop!

MEET CREEP E. CATERPILLAR

Creep E. Caterpillar may not move fast, but he gets the job done.
Round up some pals and try out Creep E.'s method of locomotion for yourself.

1 Set up a starting line and a finish line, about 4 m (12 ft.) apart, with a clear course between them.

2 Line up the players, one behind the other, at the starting line.

3 The first three people represent the three segments of the caterpillar's thorax. Have the second and third people in line put their hands on the hips of the person in front of them. Each thorax segment has a pair of true legs (see right). Each pair of legs will always move together. To move forward, a player will make a small, two-footed jump.

4 Loop the jump rope around the waist of the third person in line, with the ends behind her. The rope represents the part of the caterpillar between the true legs on the thorax and the prolegs on the abdomen.

Any remaining players behind the fourth person in line grab hold of the waist of the person in front. Players 4 to 8 are the abdominal sections of the caterpillar, each with a pair of prolegs.

5 Start the stopwatch. To move, caterpillars contract their soft bodies, lifting their rear-most prolegs off the ground together first. Have the last player in line jump, feet together, so his toes just nudge the heels of the player in front.

Creeper Camouflage

Caterpillars can take their time moving around, since they are often well camouflaged. Check out some of these clever disguises:

The caterpillar of a brownish moth called the Morning Glory Prominent is brown, with a few spots of green—an exact duplicate of an **oak leaf** that's about to fall to the ground.

The poplar hawk moth caterpillar resembles the **rolled-up leaf** of its favorite tree.

Even a very hungry bird would think twice before gobbling up this bit of **bird droppings**. But, psst—it's really a scalloped hook-tipped moth caterpillar!

It's no mystery how the **twig caterpillar** got its name. When threatened, it freezes into an upright pose that looks just like the real twig nearby.

The Wavy-lined Emerald caterpillar camouflages itself by sticking bits of the **flowers** that it eats onto its back.

As soon as the second-to-last person in line feels the player behind him brush his body, he moves by making a two-footed jump. (The player holding the rope should just jump one step's worth, not all the way to the next player.) Once the third person in line senses the fourth one jump, she can hop forward. Repeat with each player in line jumping in turn until the first player moves ahead.

6 Repeat the entire sequence, beginning each new step forward with the rear player, until all of the players cross the finish line.

7 Check how long it took for the complete caterpillar to travel the distance. Does that time seem slow or fast to you?

Are Your Legs True?

Caterpillars have three sets of true legs and up to five sets of prolegs. True legs have joints. They also have clawed ends that enable them to grab onto branches and grip food. The prolegs are fleshy and sticky, with lots of tiny hooks on the bottom that work like Velcro. The prolegs enable the caterpillar to stick upside down to the undersides of leaves or branches.

FLY HiGH, FLY!

Look up in the sky. It's a bird! It's a plane! No—it's a winged insect!

Starting a Flap

How does a fly at rest get its wings to start flapping in the first place? By jumping, says Thomas Irving, one of the scientists who conducted a study on fly flapping. When the fly jumps, moving air puts pressure on the wings, making them stretch. The stretching triggers a set of muscle contractions, and ta-dah! Bye-bye, fly. How do flies stop when they're ready to land? No one knows. Maybe it will be you who solves that ongoing mystery.

Check out how fast these babies can go!

Try It!

To hear how fast a fly's wings beat, catch one if you can, then listen in with this easy-to-make amplifier. Using your lightning-fast reflexes and a bug catcher (see page 61), catch a fly. Be patient. Transfer the fly into a waxed paper bag (like the one in a cereal box). Hold the end of the bag so the fly doesn't escape. Place the bag near your ear. Can you hear the very loud buzzing from inside it? The bag catches the vibrations of the wings to make the flapping easier to hear. Release the fly outside when you have finished.

A fly can beat its wings over **200 times a second**. But scientists have shown that the insect's brain doesn't control the wing flap. The wings flap automatically! How? The fly has two sets of muscle fibers that power its wings—one to flap up, the other to flap down. As one set of muscles contract, they stimulate the second set to contract, which in turn stimulate the first ones to contract again. And so on, and so on...

KEEP ON FLAPPING

Ever wonder what makes a fly fly? To learn the secret, lift the flap!

1 Cut through the roll from one end to the other, as shown. Make a second cut about 2.5 cm (1 in.) from the edge of your first cut. Remove this narrow strip from the tube.

2 Cut the index card in half vertically, to make two squarish "wings."

3 Lay the narrow strip of the roll on your work surface, curved side up (like a U). This piece represents the upper side of the fly's thorax.

4 Lay one index card half so that one edge overlaps the thorax. Tape in place. Repeat with the second half of the index card to make the second wing. Tape in place.

5 Fit the pieces of the roll back together—with the wings inserted. Tape the outside of the tube to the top of each wing

6 To make your model flap, hold the tube gently in one hand so the narrow strip (thorax) is at the top. With the other hand press down on the thorax. The wings will go up. Release the thorax and the wings will go down.

press

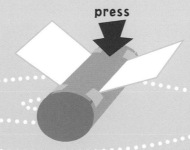

What's Going On?

Flies have two sets of muscles attached to the inside of the thorax. When one set of those muscles contracts, or shortens, it pulls the top and bottom of the thorax in. The wings go up! The second set of muscles then contracts, changing the shape of the thorax again so the wings go down. The whole process is repeated hundreds of times a second!

UP, UP, AND AWAY!

You can't just wing it if you want to fly. Insects rely on several flap-happy techniques to get airborne—and stay in flight.

LIFT-OFF MYSTERY

Ever wonder how insects can stay aloft on those teeny-tiny wings? Try this experiment to see those wings in action.

YOU'LL NEED
1 sheet of writing paper
~
ruler
~
scissors

1 Cut a strip of paper measuring 5 cm (2 in.) by 27.5 cm (11 in.).

2 Hold the narrow end of the strip just below your bottom lip. Your thumb should be under the strip and the rest of your fingers on top.

3 Blow *down* on the strip. Amazingly, the paper strip will lift *up*!

What's Going On?
The paper strip reacts to air moving across its surface the same way as an insect's wing does. It lifts. That's thanks to Bernoulli's principle, which states that as moving fluids speed up, their pressure decreases. Air, interestingly enough, is a fluid (it flows), so Bernoulli's principle applies. Before you blew across the strip, the air pressure on both sides of the paper was the same. When you blew along the top of the paper, the air pressure on that side went down. The air on the underside didn't change, so its pressure suddenly became greater than on the top. Since the pressure on the top side wasn't great enough to press down against the pressure underneath the paper, it rose up!

WHAT'S THAT BUZZ?

Flies do it. Bees do it. Buzz, that is. When they flap their wings, the vibration of their wings and thorax makes an unearthly sound. You can make a device to mimic their vocal vibrato.

YOU'LL NEED

rubber band
~
a small book
~
2 pencils
~
paper

1 Wrap the rubber band around the width of the book. It should be tight.

2 Slip the pencils between the book and the rubber band. Push them to opposite edges of the book so that the rubber band is slightly raised from the surface.

3 Hold the paper in one hand with the corner just above the rubber band. With a finger on your other hand, twang the rubber band.

4 While the rubber band is still moving, gently touch the edge of the paper, close to the corner, to the surface of the rubber band. Repeat several times until you hear the loud buzz!

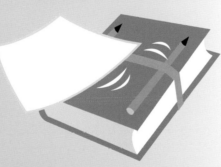

What's Going On?

As the insect flies, the thorax moves, causing a vibration. That vibration causes the bug's wings to also vibrate. You've heard this movement of the wings—it's that familiar buzzing sound. When you touch the paper to the twanged rubber band, the paper acts like the wings do when the thorax vibrates, sounding like an insect's buzzzzzzz.

In the Key of Bee?

Put a variety of insects together and you just might hear a "Symphony in Bee." Scientists have found that each flying insect species buzzes its own distinctive song, and at the same pitch. The pitch an insect makes can also tell you about its mood or state! For example, an active, healthy honeybee's wings beat at around 435 times per second—producing the same soundwave frequency as the musical note A. But when that same honeybee is tired, its wings slow down to 326 beats per second, buzzing the musical note E. Houseflies flap at a frequency that hits the note of F. Mosquitoes might chime in by buzzing in D.

FEATS OF FLIGHT

Who are the true kings and queens of insect flight? Monarch butterflies may not be the fastest, but they sure fly the farthest. Every autumn, monarch butterflies from the eastern half of North America migrate thousands of kilometres to wintering grounds in Mexico.

FLUTTER HERE

Butterflies feed on a sweet liquid in flowers called nectar. You can make artificial nectar and attract butterflies with your sweetness. You'll get the best results if you do this in the summertime.

YOU'LL NEED

1 L (4 cups) water

~

250 mL (1 cup) sugar

~

pot

~

mixing spoon

1 Pour the water into your pot, then add the sugar.

2 Get an adult to help you with this step. Heat the mixture, stirring until the sugar has dissolved. The mixture can be stored in the refrigerator for one week.

To make a butterfly nectar feeder, place your nectar in a shallow dish, such as a plant saucer or pie plate. Fill the dish with the nectar. Place a bright yellow or orange kitchen scouring pad in the plate (the color will attract the butterflies, and the pad will give them a place to perch). Place your feeder at a level just above the nearest flowers. You can stand it on an upturned flowerpot or a tree stump.

Winging It

Butterflies' wings don't just look fancy, they also perform some very fancy in-flight maneuvers. A study done at Oxford University in England trained red admiral butterflies to fly toward a fake flower that was positioned at the end of a wind tunnel. Scientists let wisps of smoke into the chamber so they could see how the butterflies' wings moved through the air. They snapped thousands of pictures to analyze.

The scientists discovered that butterflies use many different techniques to stay aloft during each flight. They easily switch from one to the other, sometimes at every stroke! The scientists were amazed by the insects' talents. They said that if human beings could figure out how the flutter-butters do it, it would cause "a revolution" in aeronautics.

Flying to Far-Flung Places

Millions of monarch butterflies make the 3,000 km (1,865 mi.) autumn trek to Mexico, from as far north as the boreal forests of Canada. In late February, the butterflies that have survived the winter then travel north, to Texas, Louisiana, and Florida. There, the butterflies lay eggs—up to 100 for every female—and die. When the hatchlings mature in early spring, they begin flying back north, searching for milkweed on which to lay their eggs along the way. Most adult butterflies live two to five weeks. But the monarch butterflies that mature in late July and August don't die so quickly. Instead, they begin the migration back to Mexico, a journey that will take six months or more to complete!

CANADA

Boreal Forest

UNITED STATES

Texas Louisiana

Florida

MEXICO

THE INSECTO-FILES

AMAZING BUG FACTS

A company in Canada has come up with a way to use the **venom from ant bites and bee stings** to power fuel cells! The mini-power sources can be used to recharge cell phones and digital cameras.

In 1999, astronauts on the Space Shuttle were introduced to their newest colleagues: four **ladybugs**. Along with some leaves and their favorite food (aphids), the ladybugs joined the crew to participate in some gravity experiments. The beetles—named John, Paul, Ringo, and George, after the musical group the Beatles—did very well in space.

Buzzing is not the only sound bees can make. **Queen bees** also toot, pipe, and quack! Virgin queens produce a toot sound as soon as they emerge from the pupae as adults. It announces to the hive that a new queen has hatched. Piping is the sound the queen makes to calm distressed workers. And a queen quacks when workers hold her captive in her cell to prevent her from attacking other queens. The queen's quack gets louder and louder until she is finally released to do battle.

QUACK! QUACK!

TOOT!

Hey, this footlong sub sandwich is only 11 inches long!

Wasps are experts at geometry. They build their nests using perfectly uniform hexagon cells. How do wasps know how to make each cell exactly the right size and shape? They use their antennae both as rulers and protractors. The length of the antennae helps determine the size of each cell. As a wasp builds, it constantly touches its antennae to the cell walls. Depending on what its antennae feel, the wasp knows when to turn and at what angle it should build the next cell wall!

MASTER BUILDERS

Termites are the architects of the insect world. They build huge, complex nests that can be home to a colony of more than a million workers. The nest includes nurseries, the royal chamber for the queen, and fungus gardens that provide food.

Never Lonely

A termite colony is made up of different groups, or castes, that each perform certain jobs. The queens and kings are the only individuals that mate and produce young. Workers are the main termite caste. They find and store food, look after the nymphs (young), maintain the nest, and defend the colony. The soldier caste is responsible for protecting the colony. They have stronger exoskeletons than the rest of the colony, and extra-large jaws. Some are equipped with holes, or nozzles, in their heads that can spray nasty chemicals at attackers.

Termite workers and soldiers are usually completely **blind**!

Many termites build massive mounds above their underground nests. A mound made by African termites known as *Macrotermes bellicosus* can be as high as a 3-story building! It can take a colony of termites **eighty years** to build one.

HOME SWEET HOME

MOUND CLIMATE CONTROL

Termites' mounds are impressive structures made of mud and termite saliva that tower above the nest. The mounds maintain a constant temperature, and control the amount of humidity in the nest. Create your own model mound to learn the secret of their cool, clever construction.

YOU'LL NEED

large garbage bag

~

empty toilet paper roll

~

6 pencils

~

2 thermometers

~

scissors

~

ruler

~

strong tape

~

string

~

pen

~

paper

1 Cut a hole in the middle of the bottom of the bag, just big enough for the toilet paper roll to fit through.

2 Stick the roll through the opening, leaving about 2.5 cm (1 in.) sticking out. Gather the bag and tape it securely to the tube.

3 In a sunny area outside, hold the tube at the top and use the string to hang the bag from a pole, wall, or branch. The open end of the bag should touch the ground.

4 Spread out the open end of the bag. Use the pencils as stakes to stick the bag into the ground.

5 Check that the temperature reading on the two thermometers is the same.

6 Lay one of the thermometers on the ground inside the bag. Tape the second thermometer vertically to the inside of the toilet paper tube.

7 After an hour, check and record both temperature readings.

8 Repeat every hour for several hours while the sun is still out. Which shows a higher average temperature, the one inside the bag or outside?

What's Going On?

The sun heats the air inside the bag. Hot air rises, so the heated air goes up the toilet paper roll. It drives the temperature inside the roll up. As hot air is drawn away, the air under the bag, close to the ground, stays cool.

Termites' bodies produce lots of heat. However, the insects need the nest to maintain a temperature of about 30°C (86°F). Without a way to get rid of the heat that builds up inside, the termite colony would literally bake to death!

That's why termites build mounds that operate like your tented bag. The mounds surround vertical chimneys. The chimneys let heat rise up and out through the thin soil at the top.

Meanwhile, fresh, cool air enters through openings on the mound's sides. It then flows down into the nest, pushing warmer air up and out. This natural air-conditioning keeps the nest within about one degree of its ideal temperature, even when it is much hotter or colder outside.

The mound's air channels also bring in oxygen and get rid of waste products like carbon dioxide.

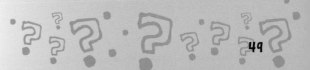

THE ANTS GO MARCHING

Like termites, wasps, and bees, ants are social insects.
This means that they live and work in colonies with other members of their species.

ON THE TRAIL

Ants communicate information by leaving a trail wherever they go. Do this activity to uncover the ants' ingenious method. (Choose a warm, dry day for best results.)

YOU'LL NEED

large sheet
of poster board

~

4–8 small rocks

~

6 crackers

~

masking tape

~

binoculars

~

watch or clock

~

paper and pencil
for recording findings

1 Draw a table on your paper like the one shown at right.

2 Locate an ant hill in your neighborhood. Caution: get help from an adult to make sure the nest is not a fire ant nest.

3 Place the poster board on the ground, with one narrow end near the ant hill. Stick a long strip of masking tape across the middle of the board, from one long edge to the other. Weight down the corners with stones to hold it.

4 Crumble one cracker. Make a pile with the crumbs about 7.5 cm (3 in.) from a corner that is farthest from the nest.

5 Crumble two more crackers and make a larger pile with the crumbs at the other far corner of the board.

6 Crumble the remaining three crackers to make the largest pile at the center of the far edge of the board.

7 Choose a spot where you can observe through the binoculars, but your presence will not disturb the ants.

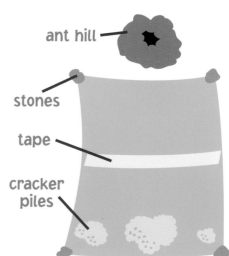

ant hill

stones

tape

cracker
piles

8 Watch what happens. Do any ants come out of the nest? How long does it take for the first ant to find one of the cracker piles? Does it head to the crumbs in a straight line, or in a random zigzag? Which pile was it?

9 Observe the behavior of the first ant to find the crackers. Does it take a crumb back to the nest? What does it do with its antennae? Its abdomen? Record your observations on your table.

10 Continue to observe the nest. Record how long it takes for the second, third, and fourth ants, etc. to find the crackers. Observe their behavior. Record whether they are carrying crumbs to the nest.

11 When a large number of ants have successfully found the crumbs, peel off the masking tape running across the board.

12 Continue observing the ants and recording your findings. Do the ants still behave as they did before you removed the tape? How long does it take until the same number of ants have found their way to the crumbs?

Ant #			
motion before finding crumbs: straight or zigzag path?			
length of time to find the crumbs			
which pile?			
carrying crumbs?			
length of time to return to nest			
type of motion: straight or zigzag path?			
notes			

What's Going On?

When foraging ants leave the nest, they lay down a chemical scent trail to find their way back. The scent is secreted from the rear of the ant's abdomen. You may have observed the ants dragging their "tails." They were laying the trail.

The ants' smell receptors are on their antennae. Did you notice the ants touching the ground with their antennae as they crossed the board? They were using their antennae to sniff for food or a scent trail.

When an ant smelled the crackers, it headed in their direction. When it reached the food, it probably ate a small bit. Then it brought some of the crumbs back to the nest in a special stomach, called a crop.

At the nest, the ants communicate that they have found food. Now more ants go out for food. They follow the scent trails laid down by the first group. The new ants add their own scent to the trails, strengthening the most popular pathways. That's why, eventually, you'll see a single straight line of ants marching to the preferred food along the same route.

When you removed the tape strip, you interrupted the scent trail. In time, the ants would make a new one.

BUSY BEES

Bees are some of the most important insects in the world.
Since they pollinate most food crops, they are a key part of the global food web.

Land ahoy!

Moving Hives

The familiar honeybee is not native to North America. It's a European insect that was highly valued in the Old World. European bees' honeycombs were collected both for their sweet and **nutritious honey**, and for their **wax**, which was used to make clean-burning candles. When the first European colonists came to North America, they were disappointed to discover that their new home had no native honeybees. The local, wild bee species produced neither honey nor wax. How would the colonists light their homes, or obtain honey to sweeten their food? In 1621, colonists at Jamestown, Virginia, solved the problem by importing European honeybee hives to the New World. In time, the European honeybee transformed the North American continent, making large-scale agriculture possible through efficient pollination of plants.

Individual worker bees only live for about **a month**. Their jobs are so demanding, they just wear out!

BE A BEE

Do you have the endurance and agility to collect enough nectar to make like a bee and make your share of honey? To find out, play this game.

1 Assign one player to be the scorekeeper for each round. Decide what your target score will be. For example, you may decide the winner is the "bee" who collects 5 mL (1 tsp.) of nectar first.

2 Place the cups of water and eye droppers at a starting line. The water represents nectar. The eyedroppers represent the bees' honey stomach.

3 Place the medicine cups at the finishing line about 3 m (10 ft.) away from the start. The medicine cups represent the hives. Make sure each player has a clear path between his or her water and medicine cup.

4 At the count of 3, the bees fill their droppers with water from their cups. They then run to the opposite end of the room and squirt the dropper into their "hives."

5 Each player continues running back and forth until all the players have filled the target amount in the medicine cup. Meanwhile, the scorekeeper records how many trips each player makes to his or her cup. The winner is the player who reached the target amount with the fewest number of trips. Play at least one more round so the scorekeeper gets a chance to be a bee!

YOU'LL NEED

2 or more friends

~

plastic eyedroppers
(one for each friend)

~

plastic medicine cups,
measured in millilitres or teaspoons
(one for each friend)

~

cups of water (one
for each friend)

~

paper and pencil for
recording scores

What's Going On?

To make 0.5 kg (1 lb.) of honey, bees have to collect nectar from two million flowers. Each bee only makes about 0.4 mL ($\frac{1}{12}$ tsp.) of honey during its lifetime. Flying at an average speed of 24 km (15 mi.) per hour, bees make ten trips a day and work twelve hours each shift. A lot of work for not a lot of honey!

A HIVE OF ACTIVITY

Don't discount them as party animals just because they are called "social."
The social insects—bees, wasps, ants, and termites—seem to have superpowers beyond
the scope of ordinary mortals. Incredible technology, awesome strength, and
unyielding loyalty make them practically invincible.

Wasps: Masters of Invention

During the 18th century, naturalist René de Réaumur was walking in the woods when he observed a wasp chewing on wood, then spitting out the mush to form its nest. It just so happened that, at that time, there was a dire shortage of rags across Europe. Europeans made paper from rags, so that meant there was a serious shortage of paper, too. Réaumur saw that the **wasp's nest resembled paper** and he wondered if he could learn to make paper by watching the wasps. And he did just that. Thanks to Réaumur, most paper today is manufactured according to the wasps' tried-and-true method.

BEE IS FOR BUILDER

Find out why bees are the efficient builders of the insect world.

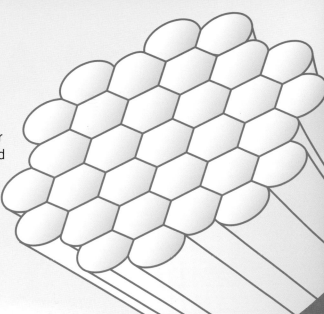

YOU'LL NEED

about 30 drinking straws

~

3–4 thick rubber bands

1 Take a look at one straw. What shape is it? (A cylinder.) What is the shape of the opening at each end? (A circle.)

2 Grasp as many straws as you can in your fist, and squeeze them together tightly. Wrap the rubber band around to hold them in place, making them as closely packed as possible.

3 Now look at the ends of the straws. What shape are they now?

What's Going On?

If you squeezed the straws together tightly enough, the straw ends should look like hexagons (flat six-sided shapes). The whole straw becomes a shape called a hexagonal prism (a 3-D shape with hexagons at both ends, joined by six rectangles).

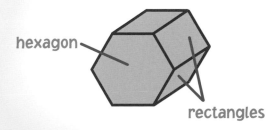

hexagon

rectangles

Why does this happen? Check out these pictures: triangles, squares, and hexagons can fill a space without leaving any gaps between them.

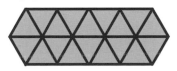

Circles cannot. They leave gaps between.

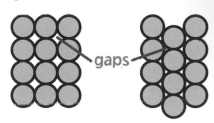

gaps

Squeezing the straws together forces the gaps to disappear, and hexagons to appear in their place. Of the three shapes, hexagons surround larger spaces best. Turn the page to find out why this geometry fact benefits the bees.

LAZY BEES?

You've just found out that hexagons are great shapes for zapping gaps. So are you wondering why bees would care? Wonder no longer, read on...

Saving Energy

Bees build the cells in their hives using **wax**. Wax takes a lot of energy to produce. The bees can save energy if they make a lot of cells using the least amount of wax. Building cells in hex-shapes is perfect for this. Bees may not be math experts, but they do take advantage of a simple rule of nature: use the *fewest materials* and the *smallest amount of energy* possible to get the job done.

The honeycombs' cells are **tilted** with the open end slightly up so that honey doesn't drip out!

You're Getting Warmer....

Bees prefer warm flowers to cold ones, say researchers at Cambridge University. Bees can even use a flower's color to predict its temperature before they land! Why would a flower's temperature be important? It takes a lot of energy for a bee to keep its body warm. Taking in chilly nectar uses up more of a bee's energy than warm nectar does.

Copying Nature

Man-made materials also display "hexagonal close packing." Next time you see some **styrofoam packaging**, take a close look at its texture. Can you see that it is made up of hexagons packed closely together? Telephone and internet cables are also made up of hexagonal fibers. That shape enables manufacturers to make thinner cables, using less raw materials.

How do bees measure their hives? They use **their bodies** as rulers and form living chains by holding on to each other's legs.

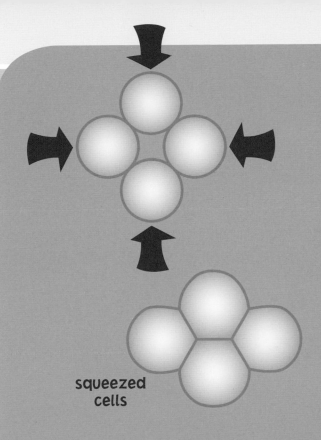

squeezed
cells

Happy Bees

A beehive is a sweet design by nature, designed to hold as much honey as possible. Here's how it works: worker bees begin to build the hive by forming small tubes of wax. The tubes are the same shape as straws. The bees continue building more tubes, putting them as close together as possible. Remember how circles leave gaps? Those gaps, inside a beehive, are wasted space. They don't hold honey. Wasted work means wasted energy! Luckily for the bees, wax is soft. As more waxy tubes are added, their soft cells get squeezed together, closer and closer, just like the straws. The wax tubes are **transformed into hexagonal prisms**, and the gaps between them disappear! Hexagon-shaped storage cells use less wax and hold more honey than any other shape container. Less wax + more honey = happy bees.

Try It!

If you look around, you'll find other examples of tightly packed circles becoming hexagons in many other places. For example, bubbles of the same size will morph into hexagons when smushed closely together. Use a straw to blow lots of small bubbles in a glass of milk or other liquid. Look at them carefully (a magnifying glass might help). Is each bubble a roughly hex-shaped ball? Check out a sinkful of dish detergent or the foam in your bubble bath, too!

DOING THE BEE DANCE!

Bees have a keen sense of smell and sharp color vision. They find food by using both finely developed senses. But how do they communicate that information to other bees in their hive?

SAY IT WITH DANCE

Can you and your friends communicate using dance steps? Bees do! Make like a bee and lead a friend to a hidden treasure.

YOU'LL NEED

a friend

~

a "treasure"
(an object that
can be hidden)

~

pen and paper

1 Decide together what your "dance language" will be. You can use these steps, or make up your own:

- **3 jumps in a row:** go straight ahead
- **shimmy:** turn left
- **spin:** go right
- **point to the sky while tapping your left foot:** look higher
- **point to your right toe repeatedly:** look lower
- **flap your arms:** you're very close!

2 Once you've got your secret language down, choose who will hide the treasure and who will try to find it.

3 The hider will hide the treasure somewhere in the room, then direct the seeker to its location using only dance steps as instructions. Once the treasure's been found, switch roles and play again.

Language Barrier

Bees, like people, speak different languages. And just like people, bees without a common language have trouble understanding each other. The result? A hive of trouble! Italian honeybees use a waggle dance when the food source is 35 m (115 ft.) from the hive. Austrian bees, on the other hand, use the waggle dance only when food sources are more than 80 m (260 ft.) away. When Italian bees and Austrian bees were mixed into the same hive, World War Bee almost erupted. The bees could not understand each other and there was mass confusion in the hive!

I Smell Like I Belong Here

Each bee colony also has its own special scent. When bees search for a new location to start a hive, they mark the site with their scent even before they start to build. Later on, that scent acts as a password into the hive. If an unrelated bee without the correct scent tries to enter the hive, guard bees at the entrance sting it to death! When a bee stings, it releases another scent that lets other bees know the hive is in danger. That smell makes the rest of the bees start stinging, too!

"Talking" Bee

Austrian scientist Karl von Frisch performed the first studies that discovered bees' ingenious method of communication. He built a special hive that he could observe through one glass side. He noticed that when bees returned to the hive, they performed a ritual—a series of movements he called "dances." After careful study, von Frisch decoded the mysterious language of the bees. The table below shows the dance steps and meanings he observed.

Food source is within 25 m (80 ft.) of the hive	Do "round" dance
If food is particularly yummy	Change directions regularly, act excited
Food source is more than 100 m (330 ft.) from the hive	Do "waggle" dance
To tell how far away	Increase length of straight run during dance
To give more information about how far away	Increase number of waggles
To tell direction of food source	Orient dance in correct angle from the sun
To describe quality of food	Increase tempo of dance, and number of repetitions of each step as food quality improves. Add high frequency buzzing song to dance.
Food source is between 25 m (80 ft.) and 100 m (330 ft.) from the hive	Perform "sickle" dance, a crescent-shaped blend of round and waggle dances
To encourage more bees to collect food	Do "vibration" dance: grab another bee with your front legs, then vibrate or shake your body vigorously

iNSPECT AN iNSECT

The best way to learn about insects is to study them firsthand. Make these low-tech, high-performance tools for best results.

MAGNIFYING BUG VIEWER

For some close-up face time with an insect, build this simple but effective viewer.

YOU'LL NEED

magnifying glass

~

clear, soft plastic disposable cup with removable lid

~

ruler

~

marker

~

scissors

~

duct tape or other strong tape

1 Place a small object on a table and look at it through the magnifying glass. How high above the object do you need to hold the lens for the object to be in focus? Use your ruler to measure this distance, for example, 7.5 cm (3 in.).

2 Remove the lid from the cup and stand the empty cup upside down on your table. Using your ruler, measure the same distance from the table on the cup. Mark it on the cup.

3 Ask an adult for help with this step. Poke a hole through the mark with your scissors. Cut off the closed end of the cup, as straight as you can. Poke a few air holes in the sides of the cup.

4 Lay the magnifying glass on the cut end of the cup. Tape it in place.

5 To observe a bug, put it into the cup and replace the lid. Stand the cup upside down on the table so you can look at the bug through the magnifier.

6 Release the bug when you have finished studying it.

TOUCHLESS BUG CATCHER

Squeamish about touching mysterious wiggly critters? No need to be with this ingenious hands-free specimen collector.

YOU'LL NEED

drinking straw
~
2.5 cm (1 in.) square of gauze
~
clear, soft plastic disposable cup with removable lid
30 cm (12 in.)

clear aquarium tubing,
1.25 cm (½ in.) in diameter
~
craft knife or scissors

clear tape
~
low temperature glue gun (optional)

1 Cut the straw so you have a segment that measures about 7.5 cm (3 in.) in length. Discard the remaining length of straw or use for another purpose.

2 Wrap the gauze square over one end of the straw. Tape in place.

3 Get an adult to help you with this step. Using the tip of the craft knife or the pointy end of the scissors, poke a hole in the bottom of the cup.

4 Stick the gauze-covered end of the straw through the hole in the bottom of the cup. Tape in place. (If you are using a glue gun, have an adult glue the straw in place.) Make sure there are no openings around the straw that air can pass through.

5 Put the lid on the cup. Stick the aquarium tubing through the hole in the lid. Glue or tape the tubing in place as you did with the straw.

6 To catch a bug, place the open end of the tubing as close to the bug as you can without disturbing it. Make sure the bug is small enough to fit through the tube! Place the straw in your mouth and inhale sharply, as if you were sucking juice from a straw. When you breathe in, it lowers the air pressure inside the cup. The bug is pulled into the cup by the stream of air rushing in to fill up the space! Don't worry: the gauze over the straw will prevent the bug from swooshing into your mouth. Remember to return the specimen to the same place you found it when you have finished your observation.

SCIENCE CONCEPTS

You probably thought this book was just loads of fun. But, of course, it was loaded with lots of great science, too. Here is a list of scientific topics and experiments covered in *The Insecto-files*.

List of Experiments You Can Do

Answers

Getting the Bug Basics, page 6: 1–C, 2–B, 3–H, 4–F, 5–I, 6–D, 7–E, 8–A, 9–G. **Spot the Fakers, page 7:** the red-winged bug is the only bug shown that has six legs, three body parts, and two antennae—the three traits shared by all insects. **The Dine and Dash, page 9:** Gus the Grasshopper likes to bite off bits of solid food, like the edge of your cracker. He chomped the picnicker's bread. Fiona the Fly prefers sweet, liquidy foods, like your honey. She lapped up the picnicker's honey and jam. Avidia the Aphid uses her pointy proboscis to pierce skinned foods that have juicy liquids inside, like your juice box. She stabbed and slurped the picnicker's grapes. Lefty the Lepidoptera likes to suck up liquids through her straw-shaped proboscis. She drank the picnicker's juice.

INDEX